Christianity in 10 Minutes

Christianity in 10 Minutes

Brian Mountford

Winchester, U.K.
New York, U.S.A.

First published in 2006 by O Books; an imprint of
John Hunt Publishing Ltd., The Bothy, Deershot Lodge,
Park Lane, Ropley, Hants, SO24 0BE, UK
office@johnhunt-publishing.com
www.O-books.net

Distribution in:

UK
Orca Book Services
orders@orcabookservices.co.uk
Tel: 01202 665432
Fax: 01202 666219
Int. code (44)

USA and Canada
NBN
custserv@nbnbooks.com
Tel: 1 800 462 6420
Fax: 1 800 338 4550

Australia
Brumby Books
sales@brumbybooks.com
Tel: 61 3 9761 5535
Fax: 61 3 9761 7095

New Zealand
Peaceful Living
books@peaceful-living.co.nz
Tel: 64 7 57 18105
Fax: 64 7 57 18513

Singapore
STP
davidbuckland@tlp.com.sg
Tel: 65 6276
Fax: 65 6276 7119

South Africa
Alternative Books
altbook@global.co.za
Tel: 27 011 792 7730
Fax: 27 011 972 7787

Design: Jim Weaver Design, Basingstoke

ISBN 1 905047 09 6

A CIP catalogue record for this book is available from the British Library.

Printed in Great Britain by Ashford Colour Press Ltd.

Contents

Foreword

Christianity in 10 Minutes could not have been published at a better time. To explain the true nature for the basis of Christian beliefs is a contribution of no mean importance in an era when some have sought to hijack Christianity and subvert the morals of Jesus to advance particular political agenda and economic gains. This daily misappropriation of Christianity drives the world toward a more intensified and, perhaps irretrievable religious divide in the clash of civilizations. In the United States we wear religion on our sleeve and daily bolster our political and personal economic fortunes by exploitation of the simple and innocent who have little earthly pleasure, but harbor great faith in the promise of the hereafter.

In the face of this use of Christianity, Canon Brian Mountford, the Vicar of St Mary's, Oxford, UK, relies on the New Testament to deliver cogent explanations of Christian belief. He identifies the essentials of Christian truth that transcend material reality. In doing so, he aids those with a simplistic belief in inerrancy, explaining that to believe in Jesus and to be a Christian does not require that you accept all the tenets of all the churches that over the centuries have imposed a gloss over his teachings. Instead, Canon Mountford suggests how the story of Jesus alone can change your life and provide comfort, strength and solace.

According to Canon Mountford, to attain this end requires, foremost, adherence to Jesus' reply to the lawyer who asked, "What must I believe?" to which Jesus responded with the golden mean: "Love God and one's neighbor." This guide provides stability of values and beliefs for those who are tossed about by the turbulence of the winds of change and uncertainty of this modern age.

Professor Kern Alexander
University of Illinois, Urbana-Champaign

Acknowledgements

The publishers and author would like to acknowledge, with thanks, the following photographic sources.

The Ashmolean Museum of Art and Archaeology, Oxford
– p2, Virgin and Child, studio of Giotto di Bondo; p7, Crucifixion/lamentation

Benny Gool – p24, Desmond Tutu

www.HolyLandPhotos.org – p10, The Peirene Fountain at Corinth

Sampson Lloyd – p40, St Paul's Cathedral

Angela Palmer – p3, barbed wire; p23, glass tower

SMV Sunday School – p33

Other photographs courtesy of the author

Starting Point

How do you learn about Christianity? Many people think they need a checklist of essential beliefs to tick off. Here are the facts and these are the steps you must take, and there are books and videos that try to meet this need. I can see their worth, but I don't use them. I don't think they do justice either to the intellectual depth of the Christian faith or its emotional power. For me, Christianity is essentially a story, and being a Christian is a response to it. This is not to downplay its "truth". Facts are not the only truth. Physicists today say that there is nothing that is materially real that we can claim as absolutely true. And whatever you think about physics and the nature of reality, no one in the world lives as if facts and objects were all that mattered.

All human life is construed by story telling. We all make sense of our lives in relation to our personal history, our childhood, family, community, and the traditions of our nation. We draw on our inheritance, both learned and genetic, we create our own goals in life, we develop relationships, we're affected by the media, and we create our own stories. It could be said that we *inhabit* our stories, we live in them, and so it is with our religions, with Christianity.

The best introduction to the Christian story is to read Mark's Gospel from beginning to end – it doesn't take very long – and to discover the wow factor that made people think that Jesus might be the Son of God. Combine this with the instinctive sense that God touches your life and you've got it. God is the biggest truth we know, Jesus its best expression.

The Archbishop of Canterbury, Rowan Williams, puts it well, discussing with *His Dark Materials* author, Philip Pulman, how Christianity is a narrative through which to interpret the meaning and purpose of life: "We are talking about a set of historical events which have, as I would say by God's guidance, become the centre of a vastly complex, imaginative scheme in which the whole of human history and human life gets reoriented".

I

What is the Story?

The Christian story is based on Jesus of Nazareth, a radical Jewish teacher of the first century, the details of whose life, such as we have them, are found in the four gospels of the New Testament. Here we read about a remarkable child born to an unmarried woman in Bethlehem in Roman-occupied Palestine. His birth is heralded by angels who announce to poor shepherds the birth of a savior, and by wise men who offer, at his cradle, symbolic gifts of gold for kingship, frankincense for godliness, and myrrh for sacrificial suffering.

We hear little else about Jesus until, as a young man in Galilee, he embarks on a peripatetic ministry of teaching, healing, social protest, and miracle working,

Virgin and Child, studio of Giotto di Bondo

supported by a group of twelve followers – including four fishermen, a tax collector, and a political activist. He also has some close female followers, but they are not listed as disciples.

From the outset he is edgy and provocative. He breaks the ritual law by healing on the Sabbath and by encouraging his disciples to pluck ears of corn on the

Sabbath, a day on which no work must be done. He claims to be empowered by God and to understand God better than the theological experts. He says that it's easier for a camel to go through the eye of a needle than for the rich to enter the Kingdom of Heaven; that you must love your neighbor and your enemy as well; and go the extra mile in helping others. He hates hypocrisy, showy religion, and religious legalism, emphasizing the spirit rather than the letter of the law. His "good news" is inclusive rather than exclusive, and therefore he mixes freely with women (unusual in the male-dominated societies of the Middle East), tax collectors, and social outcasts such as lepers and the mentally ill. When his critics say that a man of God shouldn't mix with sinners, he replies that he came to call sinners, not the righteous, to repentance.

His miracles too are provocative. In healing the blind, the lame, and touching the unclean lepers to cure them, he identifies with the Jewish expectation of a Messiah. In his first sermon, in his hometown synagogue at Nazareth, Jesus applies to himself a messianic text from the prophet Isaiah, "The Spirit of the Lord is upon me, because he has anointed me to bring good news to the poor. He has sent me to proclaim release to the captives and recovery of sight to the blind, to let the oppressed go free".

The Jewish expectation of a messiah was tied up with politics as well as religion, as it is for many around the world today. Many Jews, especially the Zealots, hoped for a leader who would lead an uprising against the Romans and restore home rule: they wanted Jesus to take up their nationalistic hope. Equally, many today feel that God calls them to intervene in the politics of the world, to throw out oppressors or terrorists of whatever stripe. But he wasn't that kind of messiah. This became very clear in the last week of his life when he entered Jerusalem riding on a donkey. As John says, quoting a verse from Zechariah 9, "Your king comes humble and riding on a donkey".

During his ministry Jesus had been very aware of the dangers of acting and speaking out as he did. At a pivotal moment, in the central chapter of Mark's Gospel, he asks his disciples what public opinion has to say about him. They tell him some say he's a prophet and others even think he is John the Baptist come back from the dead. But he wants to know their own view and Peter says, "You are the Messiah". The disciples recognize God working through him. However, much to their surprise, Jesus then explains that he will suffer and be killed for his beliefs and that anyone who wants to follow him must be ready to make the same sacrifice.

The crunch event happened after his entry into Jerusalem on a donkey. He went to the Temple, the most holy and symbolic building of the Jewish nation, and overturned the tables of the moneychangers and drove out the tradesmen selling birds and animals for sacrifice. Quoting scripture, he shouted, "My house shall be called a house of prayer, but you have made it a den of thieves". This was a double provocation: by referring to "my house" he identified himself with God, which was blasphemy, and by demonstrating against temple abuse, he criticized Judaism itself, which was a kind of treason. This was sufficient to seal his enemies' determination to destroy him. One of the accusations with which he was taunted when he was crucified was that he had said he would destroy the temple made with hands, and in three days build another, not made with hands – clear-cut blasphemy as far as the Jews were concerned. The same kinds of accusations still resound around the world today. That we're not strict enough, strong enough, or supportive enough, of our traditions. We all have our present day temples.

And so, walking through the olive trees after having eaten the Passover meal with his disciples, the popular young teacher is arrested by night, betrayed by Judas, one of his disciples, and subsequently deserted by the others. He is tried before the High Priest and before Pontius Pilate, the Roman Governor, and accused of blasphemy and incitement to rebellion against Rome – a capital offence. As a consequence he was stripped and flogged before being crucified by Roman soldiers, for whom he asked God's forgiveness. The friends and family who witnessed this cruelty must have felt all hope evaporate. This, surely, was the end of his project and his idealism. At one dreadful moment he cried out, "My God why have you forsaken me", but when at last he died, the soldier standing guard said, "Surely this man was a son of God".

When his body had been taken down from the cross, he was buried by a sympathetic supporter, Joseph of Arimathea, in a tomb hewn out the rock, with a stone rolled across the opening. After his death the question of who he was, was asked even more urgently. Is he the suffering servant of Isaiah, a suffering messiah? Was his death a sacrifice for sin, like the sacrifice of a lamb at the Passover? Could his love and godliness have survived death and be living on?

There are many stories about Jesus rising from the dead. Women who take spices to the tomb find it empty; Jesus appears to Mary Magdalene in the cemetery garden; he walks with two of the disciples on the Road to Emmaus; and Paul tells us that he appeared to large groups of people at once. Whatever you make of the resurrection one fact is undeniable: that very soon after Jesus' death

people experienced his living presence, and a new religion based on his life and teachings spread rapidly round the Mediterranean Sea. Defeat is turned to victory. The religious conservatives and fanatics who fought for his execution have failed and a new quality of faith and spirituality has emerged – eternal life, new life, hope, future, and liberation.

At this crucial turning point in Christian history, namely the resurrection, it's the story that matters. Some Christians argue until they're red in the face whether a biblical event happened or didn't happen as it is told. Can you be a Christian without believing that miracles literally happened? In reality you can be a Christian whether you're a literalist or not; and there are many on both sides of that fence. In the end it's the power of the story that matters, the narrative thrust, the unavoidable sensation that something extraordinary is being revealed.

Forty days after the resurrection Jesus ascended into heaven to be reunited with God the father and ten days after that the presence of the Holy Spirit was experienced by the Apostles – a sensation like wind and fire which allowed them to speak in many languages.

2

What St Paul thinks

The first writings that we have about Jesus are those of St Paul in his letters. In the immediate aftermath of Easter, Paul was vehemently anti-Christian and indeed, was on his way to Damascus to arrest all the Christians he could lay his hands on and bring them to Jerusalem, when he had a blinding vision of God and heard a voice asking, "Saul, Saul, why do you persecute me?" As a result he became a convert and, having interpreted his vision as resurrection appearance, counted himself an apostle, along with Peter, James and John. In an astonishing u-turn he became a tireless missionary, preaching about Jesus and establishing churches in towns and cities around the Mediterranean, such as Corinth, Ephesus and Rome.

The Peirene Fountain at Corinth

Paul turns out to be not only an avid propagandist but a brilliant thinker and theologian. He asks the basic question about the meaning of Jesus' life and answers it with a display of theological fireworks.

1. God is fully present in Jesus. In the letter to the Colossians Paul says, "in him the whole fullness of deity dwells bodily".
2. God's action in Jesus brings salvation to human beings by restoring their relationship with God, which had been damaged by sin. "God was in Christ reconciling the world to himself" (2 Corinthians 5:19). Paul says it's like slaves being freed from slavery; or like charges

being dropped in a court case; or (a very Jewish imagery this) like making a new covenant with God sealed not with the blood of an animal sacrifice, but by Christ's own blood. In the first letter to the Corinthians 15:22 he says, "as in Adam all die, so in Christ will all be made alive".

3. People can't earn the right to a new relationship with God by good behavior. This comes as a free gift given by God's grace. He writes to the Galatians (Galatians 2:16) "We know that a person is justified (i.e. put in a right relationship) not by the works of the law but through faith in Jesus Christ".
4. The new life of Christ is expressed through the Church, which Paul calls "the body of Christ". The Church is comprised of people with different talents and spiritual gifts. God's presence in the Church is evident in the works of the Holy Spirit, which is particularly manifest at baptism; and Christ's continuing presence in the Church is celebrated by the memorial ceremony of the Last Supper (that Passover meal mentioned above), which Paul describes in 1 Corinthians 11 and concludes: "As often as you eat this bread and drink the cup, you proclaim the Lord's death until he comes".
5. Although salvation is not earned by good works, being a follower of Christ demands the high moral standards that are naturally rooted in God's love. Paul's most famous passage, popular at weddings, is about love.

He says in 1 Corinthians 13 that love "bears all things, believes all things, hopes all things, endures all things. Love never ends".

3

The Gospel question: who is Jesus?

The gospels were all written after Paul's letters, and they too interpret the life of Jesus; but their questions, particularly in Matthew, Mark, and Luke, appear more raw and unsophisticated.

When Jesus healed a paralyzed man, he told him that his sins were forgiven, and some of those present said, "Why does this fellow speak in this way? It is blasphemy! Who can forgive sins but God alone?" (Mark 2:7). The obvious implication of this is that Jesus reveals something of God in his character.

When Jesus stilled the storm on the Sea of Galilee,

the disciples were amazed and asked, "What sort of man is this, that even the winds and the sea obey him?" This is a rhetorical question and the assumed answer is that only God has power over nature.

In Luke's account of the trial of Jesus, Jesus is asked whether he is the Messiah. He says that there's no point answering because they wouldn't believe him anyway; then adds, "but from now on the Son of Man will be seated at the right hand of the power of God." Then they ask whether he is the Son of God, and he replies, "You say that I am." This is regarded as sufficient blasphemy to warrant the death penalty.

The fourth Gospel, St John, is less narrative in style and more disposed to making claims for Jesus rather than letting the story speak for itself. So, for example, John writes unequivocally, "God so loved the world that he gave his only Son, so that everyone who believes in him may not perish but may have eternal life".

4
How the Church responds

Ever since those early days the Church has continued to interpret the life of Jesus and to discuss its theological implications for Christians and for society in general. What should Christians believe and how should they act? It was the Church that developed the doctrine of the Trinity – the idea that God is three persons: Father, Son, and Holy Spirit – which is not a specific teaching of the Bible. The Church debated the question of how Jesus could be at the same time both God and man, and formalized its basic beliefs in the creeds. The Church also developed its moral thinking asking, for example, how Jesus' advocacy of pacifism squared with the political reality of war – a question it answered with the theory of a "just war".

The contemporary Church continues to think through similar questions: such as Christian responsibility in public life, the Christian response to changing sexual morality, the Christian response to terrorism, war and poverty, how Christianity relates to other faiths, and whether the Bible is literally or metaphorically true.

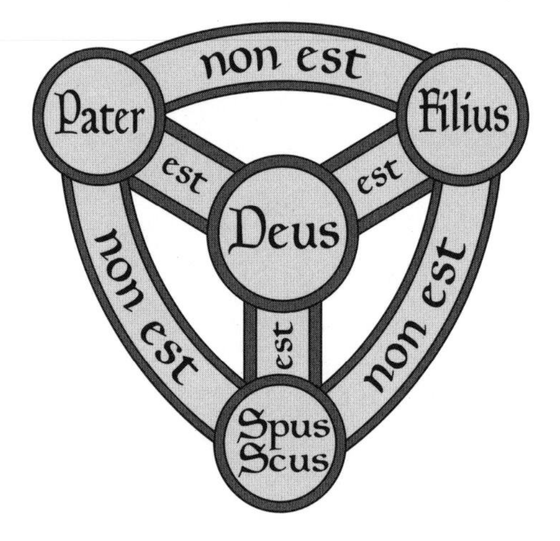

5

What must I believe?

As was suggested at the outset, being a Christian is more of an *experience* than the intellectual assent to particular beliefs. Interestingly, the way the question comes out in the gospels is not "what must I *believe*", but "what must I *do*" to inherit eternal life. A rich young man asks this question and Jesus, having established that he keeps the commandments, tells him that he must go and sell all that he has and give to the poor before he can become a follower. The gospel narrative adds: "When he heard this, he was shocked and went away grieving, for he had many possessions".

On another, more famous occasion, a lawyer asks what he must do to have eternal life and Jesus tells him that he must love God and love his neighbor as he loves himself.

When the lawyer asks for a definition of neighborliness, Jesus tells the parable of the Good Samaritan, in which a priest and a Levite, upright and religious citizens, callously ignored the plight of their fellow Jew who had been left for dead at the roadside, whereas a Samaritan "foreigner" helps him and binds up his wounds.

But still you insist, *what must I believe*? Jesus' initial reply to the lawyer about loving God and one's neighbor provides the answer. The basic belief of Christianity is that the God who reveals his nature in the life of Jesus Christ, desires human beings to try to live like Christ. That is the basic creed and all other arguments about belief, such as the Trinity, the virgin birth, or the inspiration of the Bible, are secondary to that.

Much of what we think of as Christianity today was developed centuries after the death and resurrection of Jesus. Some Christians say you have to take the whole process and accept it all, lock stock and barrel, to be a Christian. And it clearly helps to be part of the Christian community, the Church, if you can accept one or other of the main traditions, because belief is often strengthened by worship and particularly by discussion of religious ideas with other people.

6

What is Faith?

Faith is different from belief and it can be helpful to make the distinction. Faith is that underlying, instinctive response to God that comes from experience. It is not unusual for people to share a common faith but to believe different things about how the experience is to be interpreted, especially as we have seen in matters of biblical interpretation and moral judgment. Take two Christians who share the instinctive faith that the life of Christ reveals what God is like: one believes the resurrection was physical, the other believes that it was spiritual; one believes the Church should have bishops, the other doesn't; one believes abortion is always wrong, the other sees a moral justification; one believes priests should be celibate, the other does not.

These differences of belief can and do cause major divisions between Christians, reflected in the way the Church is separated into different denominations, and at worst in sectarian divides such as in Northern Ireland.

But according to the most basic teaching of the New Testament, St Paul's second theological insight above, Christian salvation isn't achieved by being able to tick off a list of creedal statements to see what kind of Christian you are. That exercise never achieves anything very useful. According to Paul and Martin Luther, the Church stands or falls, by the principle of justification by grace through faith. This is understood, as the theologian John Barton states, as "one's sense of being grasped by God through an act which owes everything to God and nothing to one's own efforts, and which one appropriates by mere assent, not through anxious striving". Christian faith begins with an encounter with the God, not necessarily in an overwhelming conversion experience, but very often as a gradual dawning of the light, sometimes endlessly repeated throughout one's Christian life.

What follows in the Christian life has to be a careful working out of the implications of faith, through reading of the Bible, getting to know the Christian tradition and rational reflection on these; but faith itself is enough to set a person at one with God. As Pascal said, "you would not be seeking me if you hadn't already found me".

7

How can the story change your life?

1. By putting you in the big picture.
   One big fear is that our lives don't actually mean anything and that they are merely accidental in the mind-bending process of the universe. The feeling is summed up in Shakespeare by Macbeth's forlorn view of life:

   "Life's but a walking shadow, a poor player
   Who struts and frets his hour upon the stage,
   And then is heard no more; it is a tale
   Told by an idiot, full of sound and fury,
   Signifying nothing."

The Christian story counters this by providing a coherent view of life, which has underlying purpose and is supported by a good and loving God. Our lives have meaning not simply as a result of our actions and relationships, but because we are loved by an infinite God whose love holds us in his being, like a parent holds a child in their arms. "The eternal God is your dwelling place and underneath are the everlasting arms", it says in the Old Testament – Deuteronomy 33:27. In this sense a person has eternal meaning and significance beyond the limits of their physical birth and death; they have a place in the big picture because they have a place in the eternal being of God. This is obviously a mystery, but a *mystery is to be* explored rather than explained. Few of us believe we will ever know everything. Faith is our instinct that it does make ultimate sense.

2. By offering salvation and forgiveness.

   What divides us from God is the dark, destructive side of our nature; whether it's manifest in random street violence, calculated terrorism, suicide bombing, hostage taking, the exploitation of false dreams through gambling, or men who traffic in sex slaves. Yet having chosen those extreme examples, there's always a danger of making the dark side of human nature so tabloid and dramatic that we come to believe it's only *other people* who embody dark destruction, while we look on from the outside. But every extreme act has its genesis in a less extreme experience: the temper tantrum, the sulk, the betrayal, gossip, the gloating over another's downfall, the secret act of selfishness, the untamed fantasy, the cruel word so stabbingly meant – even though we might consider these commonplaces less sinister, they are all aspects of the dark side. They alienate us from God because they spray an opaque film over goodness, they blur vision, impair judgment, inhibit us from seeing others clearly.

Those who experience guilt or alienation are likely to feel alone and cut off from God. The gulf between God and humanity, caused by the dark side, has to be bridged. All Christians believe, in some form or another, that the death of Jesus has the power, as the New Testament says, to "take away the sin of the world". It is the means of restoring the relationship between sinful people and the God of love, and to set them at one again. It is because God is present in Christ's sufferings that he is able to convince us of the inexhaustible power of his love.

The story also provides a model for human forgiveness

and bridge building. One of the best examples of this in practice is the Truth and Reconciliation movement in South Africa, which tries to heal the injuries of the apartheid years. We have to deal with what we feel about the past, including our anger. Anger might make us feel self-justification, but it doesn't draw the poison. Jesus teaches the importance of saying sorry and meaning it. Forgiveness is always costly and never cheap and easy. Suppose you steal someone's bicycle

Bishop Desmond Tutu

and after six months feel guilty and say sorry, and the offended party says that's OK, but then you still keep the bicycle. You've got to be able to give the bicycle back. Reparation is important. In Christian repentance it's important to be sorry and to make amends.
When a person accepts that God is willing to forgive them the experience is very life enhancing.

3. By providing comfort
Jesus said, "Come to me, all you that are weary and are carrying heavy burdens, and I will give you rest". (Matthew 11:8) Here he recognizes the weight of people's problems, but nowhere does he suggest that these will be magically spirited away as a result of religious faith; rather that Christianity is a resource for coping with the things that life throws up.

Another meaning for "comfort" in the Christian vocabulary is "encouragement". In the Bayeux Tapestry in France, there's a picture of a bishop encouraging his farmers to work. Underneath are the Latin words: *hic Odo episcopus* (here Bishop Odo) *baculum tenens* (holding a stick) *confortat pueros* (encourages his Squires). *confortat* is the same word as comfort, but here means "encourage" or "gives strength to". Christian faith can give strength to a person and there are many passages in the Bible where people are strengthened by God to face adversity, from Daniel in the Lion's Den to Paul in prison in Rome.

4. As a guide to prayer

   Other comforts of Christian faith are found through prayer. The gospel tells us that Jesus prayed to God throughout his life and taught his disciples a prayer that has become the basic and universal prayer for all Christians – the Lord's Prayer.

   Our Father, who art in heaven, hallowed be thy name. Thy kingdom come; thy will be done, on earth as it is in heaven. Give us this day our daily bread, and forgive us our trespasses, as we forgive those who trespass against us. And lead us not into temptation, but deliver us from evil. For thine is the kingdom, the power and the glory, for ever and ever. Amen.

5. By challenging you to fulfill your potential

   The Christian story challenges as much as it reassures; and that challenge is primarily a moral one. God has great expectations: he expects a person to give of their best but doesn't ask the impossible. As the creator he knows the potential of his creatures and does them the honor of expecting them to live up to their potential, just as a good parent does.

   Most people enjoy responding to a challenge and there are some big moral challenges on the way: such as loving others as much as one loves oneself, loving your enemy, and by putting oneself out for others – going the proverbial "extra mile" (which comes from Jesus' teaching that if a soldier forces you to carry his bag for one mile, go with him two). This includes caring for children, the weak, the sick, the poor and the politically oppressed.

But in addition to tangible good works, God expects people to have a moral disposition characterized by what Jesus calls "purity of heart".

6. By showing the rewards of a non materialistic lifestyle

It has often been said that Jesus' gospel is "Good news for the poor". The rewards of a non-materialistic lifestyle may seem a ludicrous "benefit", especially for people in the rich West. We have grown used to the worship of wealth, sexual beauty and pleasure, somehow summed up by the so-called "celebrity" culture, with associated TV shows and magazines. Many people aspire to this kind of ideal, but ultimately it is a fantasy likely to breed the dissatisfaction of envy and shallowness.

Christianity, at least, has a sense of proportion about the material world. On the one hand it affirms it, recognizing that God created it for our use and enjoyment; but on the other, sees that that the material world is the essential environment where the more deeply satisfying spiritual values of love, peace, generosity, and self-control can be developed. Jesus makes this point in the Sermon on the Mount (Matthew 6) when, having talked about how God clothes the lilies of the field, he tells his audience not to worry about food, drink or clothing – "your heavenly Father knows that you need all these things" – but to strive first for God's values, and then perhaps these other things will follow naturally. Christianity says that there are much more important things than wealth, glamour and success and that it's crazy to get eaten up by these things. This can be a great relief.

8

Is there just one true version of Christianity?

Those searching for a Christian faith naturally want a clear, unequivocal definition of Christian belief. But in fact Christianity embraces a wide variety of beliefs and practices, even though it depends on the same story and the same sacred texts. There are Baptists, Methodists, Catholics, Anglicans, Russian Orthodox, Greek Orthodox, Presbyterians, Quakers, Vineyard Churches, to name but a few. In the variety of Christian faith and practice, wealth, poverty, history, race, geography and temperament all come into play. The Church in Africa is different from the Church in England, and the Church in Holland different from the Church in America. Also there is a great fault line through Christianity dividing fundamentalists from liberals and biblical literalists from those who read the Bible as literature. Some churches have bishops, others do not; some ordain women, some do not; some are charismatic, others are not. Christianity has to be described as a series of opposites rather than one single straight and narrow *via media*.

Thus, Christianity has many strands and no single strand is the "true" Christianity, however many adherents of a particular belief think they are right. There's a joke about St Peter showing a group of new arrivals in heaven to their accommodation and as they pass the evangelical quarter (it could be the Catholic or the liberal quarter), he tells them to whisper. One member of the group asks why, and he replies, "because they think they're the only ones here".

This rich variety of interpretation of God's story is seen by some as a weakness, especially when a person is looking to find a basic faith, but most agree that the breadth of theological understanding is in fact a strength.

9
Can I believe without belonging?

People often tell me that you don't have to go to church to be a Christian – that you can "believe without belonging" – and at one level that seems fair comment. When you look at the Church's rancorous internal arguments about its institutional life (the Bible, sex and who should be ordained) and its frequent failure to address the big issues of the day, you might understand why some think religion is best kept as an individualistic experience, and prefer to go it alone. Although, in my experience, those who say that Church and being a Christian don't necessarily go together usually mean that they try to live by basic Christian moral standards in the broadest sense, but don't see that anything more is useful or required. It may also be that they have experienced going to a local church and have found it dull, or unfriendly, or out-of-date, or that their children have hated it. They can't be blamed for that, but their mistake may be that they are treating Christianity as yet another consumer product rather than a way of life.

Christianity is inescapably a community religion, interpersonal and relational, and ought never to be a private or lonely pursuit, except perhaps for the extreme situations of being stranded on a desert island or locked up in solitary confinement. But even then there is a sense of belonging to a wider community beyond the confines of immediate geography, the Communion of Saints, the aggregation of other Christians throughout the world, past and present. The prayer for All Saints Day describes the Church as a group "knit together ... in one communion and fellowship in the mystical body of Christ our Lord".

Anyone who wants to take the Christian religion seriously has simply got to give it a go and get involved with a local church and to be part of a community of people with a common purpose and common sense of service. It isn't always easy and in western Europe and many parts of the world today, involvement in a church community is now counter-cultural; that is to say, it runs against the prevailing intellectual culture and certainly against the general tide of leisure activities, when the kids have to be driven to sports fixtures and Sunday is the only free day for family visits. So the initial stages of joining can feel quite difficult and daunting. However, those who are members of a church usually find mutual support and enjoy a growing sense of belonging that can build strong loyalties and strong social commitment.

10
Worship

The primary activity of the Church is worship, when people meet together for prayer, reading of scripture, teaching, and affirmation of faith. Every Christian has a duty to worship and that is why such meetings are often called "services", implying a relationship of reverence towards a higher being.

At its best worship creates a drama that leads the imagination into God, reaching out to the transcendent, helping the worshipper to a deeper spiritual understanding. But it also functions as a public drama helping people to express the importance of memory, or their sense of seriousness, or celebration, or the turning points of life, the rites of passage such as birth, marriage and death. It is able to capture a public mood better than almost anything else, and that is why a community often turns to the Church for a liturgy to mark grief at a time of national crisis or disaster such as 9/11 or the recent loss of life in Iraq.

But worship is not one-way traffic; God also comes to the worshipper through what are called the *sacraments*, usually defined as the "outward, visible sign of inward and spiritual grace". This is the idea that God's presence can be mediated by a physical sign: the water of baptism, the bread and wine of the Eucharist, the laying on of hands at confirmation and ordination, the joining of hand and giving of a ring at marriage, and the anointing the sick and the dying with oil of unction.

Worship is also a context for thinking about theology, not only in the obvious sense that in the course of worship there might be teaching and Bible exposition, but that the words used in services (the liturgy) make theological statements: the creeds sum up belief and prayers and hymns are full of theological opinions. For example, prayers often begin with a definition of God – "Almighty God, *who forgives all who truly repent*" or, "Lord of all *power and might*, who art the *author and giver of all good things*".

The importance of retelling the Christian story is embodied in the worship pattern of many churches by following the main events of the gospels through the Sundays of the year. The table below gives the outline of how this works.

11

The Christian Year

Season	Time of Year	Celebrates
Advent	December	Anticipates the coming of Christ
Christmas	25 December	The birth of Jesus Christ in Bethlehem and adoration of the shepherds
Epiphany	6 January	The revelation to the Wise Men that Jesus is a holy child of God
Lent	February/March (varies according to the date of Easter)	A time of penitential preparation for Easter – reflecting on Jesus' forty days in the wilderness
Holy Week	The week before Easter	Recalls the events of the last week of Jesus' life, including his entry to Jerusalem, arrest, trial and crucifixion
Easter	March/April	The Resurrection of Jesus and the discovery of the empty tomb by Jesus' women followers and disciples

Season	Time of Year	Celebrates
Ascension tide	May	The Risen Christ is reunited with God by ascending into heaven
Pentecost	May	The coming of the Holy Spirit, like wind and fire upon the disciples
Trinity	June/November	Festival celebrating the belief that God is Father, Son and Holy Spirit. Followed by five months of ordinary Sundays

12

Four foundational Christian principles

The Christian story challenges the world's understanding of who and what is important. Yet in the history of Christianity, as Church and State conspired together in the acquisition of political power in Europe and America, it's subversive and prophetic insights have so often been missed – a point made by Dean Inge of St Paul's Cathedral in the early twentieth century when he said, "I hear of *empty* churches. I know of many churches that would be less *full* if the gospel were actually preached in them". That is to say, Jesus' moral challenge ought to be provocative not merely to the secular world, but to religious people as well.

Millions of people today are still asking what they must do to inherit eternal life, even if not exactly in those

St Paul's Cathedral

words, as they look for anchor points in a very relativistic and unstable world order. What are the values that ultimately matter, which might be an antidote to society's fragmentation, material obsession and discontent? Are there any absolutes that can be relied on? In principle absolutes are both dangerous and elusive; dangerous because they can lead to totalitarianism and elusive because what we think is truth can like sand easily slip through the fingers, but the following overarching moral ideas encapsulated by Christianity seem to meet the need:

1. The sovereignty of love over other virtues.
2. The priority of the spiritual over the material.
3. The importance of relationship and community.
4. The imperative to seek after truth.

The sovereignty of love over other virtues

Love is the absolutely key concept for Christianity. St Paul wrote to the Corinthians that faith, hope, and love are the ultimate virtues, and that "the greatest of these is love", and the First Letter of John says quite unequivocally that "God is love, and those who live in love live in God, and God lives in them". By that account, love is the nature of reality, the pure essence of being. But it's a totally selfless quality and is to be distinguished from the more self-regarding, erotic love that provides the usual meaning of the word.

There's a danger, of course, of making Christian love so idealistic that it seems unobtainable and unconnected with normal human experience. St Augustine and Martin Luther are a bit guilty of this and realistically there needs to be a balance between the two. While it's true that selfishness is the enemy of spiritual understanding and development, it's also a well attested psychological fact that crude self-negation leads to lowering of self-esteem and that you can't love someone else adequately if you hate or despise yourself. So, surrender of self can endanger personal development. For example, you would scarcely nurture a child by telling her that her sense of self was unimportant, because what children need is affirmation to build up their self-esteem.

Similarly, a significant part of God's love for us is that he has, as it were, great expectations for us – he wants us to fulfill our potential and to be the best that we can be. The cliché that in order to love others you must learn to love yourself holds a lot of water.

Perhaps the key to the idea of Christian love is *attention to the other* – both to God and one's neighbor. When you attend deeply to another person, whether it's listening to their conversation or simply being with them, you reach out to them and, in a manner of speaking, give of yourself to them, forgetting for a moment your own needs and concentrating on theirs. As the novelist and philosopher, Iris Murdoch, put it, "Love is the proper recognition that other people actually exist".

For Christians it is similar with God; the response to God's love is openness to God. Augustine spoke of love as a motion of the soul towards God, a point embodied in one of his most famous remarks: "my soul is restless till it finds its rest in thee".

It is sometimes argued that all human love draws its energy from God's love, rather like plugging in to a power supply to draw off a current, and that this is the truth of the matter whether you know it or not. It's the same point that is made in the famous antiphon from the ceremony of the Washing of the Feet at the Mass of the Last Supper on Holy Thursday, the *Ubi Caritas Deus ibi est*, which can be translated as "'wherever charity and love are found, God is there".

The priority of the spiritual over the material

The British furniture retailer, "Courts", ran an advertisement for half-price sofas, which read: "Simple mathematics: £1799 minus £900 equals happiness".

Christianity offers a different happiness formula, 'Blessed are the poor in spirit, for theirs is the kingdom of heaven' (Matthew 5:3). Or as another translation puts it, "how blest are those who know their need of God". The person who knows their need of God will anchor their lives and priorities in the spiritual, which is what Jesus means when he says, "where your treasure is, there will your heart be also".

It has become commonplace to believe that more money, more holidays, and more cars equals more happiness. It isn't true, but it's contributed to the global warming ecological crisis and the fact that present levels of fossil fuel consumption cannot be sustained long term. The priority of the spiritual over the material leads to a theology of the environment that says because God is creator and humans are made in God's image they have the privilege to enjoy environment and a duty to honor it in a mutual and co-operative way that leads to material satisfaction.

At the anecdotal level it is interesting how many people, who have spent the first twenty years of the adult life chasing after material wealth as bankers and lawyers, find themselves in mid life wanting to live more simply and, as they say, "to give something back to the community". Not that this is more than a dream or a fond hope in many cases, but it indicates a basic recognition that acquisition of wealth is rarely as satisfying as contributing to the community.

The importance of relationship and community

When Jesus summarized the law as the love of God and neighbor, he made it clear that the beginning of morality is the sympathetic understanding of other people, trying to appreciate what it is like to be in other people's shoes. The Church recognizes the importance of inter-relationship, mutuality, and the common good by making its central act of worship the "communion" in which people symbolically share a meal together when they eat the bread and drink the wine.

This extends into social commitment and service to the community which manifests itself in helping the homeless, the sick, and the marginalized both at a local and international level, work that is undertaken by such organizations as "Christian Aid".

The imperative to seek after truth

In St John 16:13 Jesus speaks of God the Holy Spirit as the Spirit of truth. He says, "When the Spirit of truth comes, he will guide you into all the truth". In this sense, to seek after truth is to seek after God. Obviously in today's multi-cultural and pluralist society not everyone will accept that equation, but it is an equation with a history. For example, in Oxford where I live, the University motto is a phrase from the Psalms, *Dominus illuminatio mea*, the Lord is my light.

The purpose of any University, whatever one's religious or cultural point of view, must be to seek after truth, wherever that may lead, and however much the journey may break down your assumptions. It must be to throw light on every scientific and intellectual question. In the early University it was clearly believed that God was that light and that is still the essence of Christian faith, that there is an eternal mind, as the poetry of the prologue to St John's Gospel, referring to John the Baptist as the forerunner of Jesus, puts it:

"He came as a witness to testify to the light ... the true light, which enlightens everyone, was coming into the world".

But truth is also essential to love and healing, as already seen in the very title of the South African "Truth and Reconciliation Movement", which has provided a methodology for other similar healing programs. This kind of political thinking, inspired by Christianity, highlights the need for truth in both personal and international relationships – from legitimate leaders and governments as well as terrorists, if we are to progress towards peace and justice and healing in our world. This may seem to be to state the blindingly obvious, but it's a lesson that it seems extraordinarily difficult to learn.

13
Summary

I have written this short book, in the first instance, for the thousands of people who enter my ancient church in Oxford, and churches like it throughout the world, drawn by curiosity over the mystery it purports to unfold and by the sense of awe and numinous that, at its best, it is able to relate. This group of people come as tourists and pilgrims, to attend concerts and events, or drop in hesitantly at the back of a religious service, many of them hoping for an intimation holiness and a glimpse of the deep-down meaning of things. It occurs to me therefore that people engage with the Christian religion at a wide variety of levels, more or less profoundly, often by brushing up against it while visiting a church on holiday, or attending a concert at which a religious work is performed, or going to an art gallery and seeing pictures of biblical scenes and events. And what often bewilders them is that it is hard to make sense of what they see and hear because they *don't know the story*.

Last time I stood in the Sistine Chapel in Rome I met a couple struggling, without a guide book, to understand the biblical pictures on the walls around them and on Michelangelo's famous ceiling above them and when we got into conversation and I was able, from a lifetime's

experience, to explain the story behind the pictures, they said that it all "came alive" for them.

I have argued that Christianity *comes alive* through the story of Jesus Christ and that Christians live in the story and in dialogue with the story, in just the same way as everyone understands who they are by reference to their personal memories and cultural histories.

So the running order for discovering what it means to be a Christian is as follows:

1. Instinctive religious curiosity.
2. Being wowed by the narrative thrust of the gospel story.
3. Responding with faith by saying 'yes' to God.
4. Responding with action in answer to the gospel question, 'what must I do to inherit eternal life?'
5. Seeking out the Christian Community and making a commitment to it.
6. Thinking about what you believe.

And if this appeals to you and you see a way forward here, then may the Spirit go with you.